WHSmith

REVISION

Science

Mark Levesley and
Lynn Huggins-Cooper

**Age 9–10
Year 5**
Key Stage 2

Hachette UK's policy is to use papers that are natural, renewable and recyclable products and made from wood grown in sustainable forests. The logging and manufacturing processes are expected to conform to the environmental regulations of the country of origin.

Orders: please contact Bookpoint Ltd, 130 Milton Park, Abingdon, Oxon OX14 4SB. Telephone: (44) 01235 827720. Fax: (44) 01235 400454. Lines are open 9.00a.m.–5.00p.m., Monday to Saturday, with a 24-hour message answering service. Visit our website at www.hoddereducation.co.uk.

© Mark Levesley and Lynn Huggins-Cooper 2013
First published in 2007 exclusively for WHSmith by
Hodder Education
An Hachette UK Company
338 Euston Road
London NW1 3BH

This second edition first published in 2013 exclusively for WHSmith by Hodder Education.

Impression number   10 9 8 7 6 5 4 3 2 1
Year   2018 2017 2016 2015 2014 2013

All rights reserved. Apart from any use permitted under UK copyright law, no part of this publication may be reproduced or transmitted in any form or by any means, electronic or mechanical, including photocopying and recording, or held within any information storage and retrieval system, without permission in writing from the publisher or under licence from the Copyright Licensing Agency Limited. Further details of such licences (for reprographic reproduction) may be obtained from the Copyright Licensing Agency Limited, Saffron House, 6–10 Kirby Street, London EC1N 8TS.

Cover illustration by Oxford Designers and Illustrators Ltd
All other illustrations Fakenham Prepress Solutions, Fakenham, Norfolk NR21 8NN
Typeset in 16pt Folio by Fakenham Prepress Solutions, Fakenham, Norfolk NR21 8NN
Printed in Italy

A catalogue record for this title is available from the British Library.

ISBN: 978 1444 189 018

Introduction

The *WHS Revision* series

The *WHS Revision* books enable you to help your child revise and practise important skills taught in school. In the *Science Revision KS2* series, there are four science books for children aged 7–11, with one book for each year. Each book contains a series of units, which contain the same material as is most commonly taught in schools in each year. This means that throughout the year you can provide your child with appropriate essential science skills that ensure progress, continuity and development.

How to use this book

Units

This book is divided into 6 sections, each of which is split into a series of units. This means that the material can be studied in a series of easily manageable 'chunks'. Each page begins with a **Remember** section, which introduces the page and gives your child essential information. If possible, read and discuss this with your child to ensure that he or she understands it.

This is followed by the **Have a go** section – activities that help your child practise using the information effectively. By and large, your child should be able to undertake these practice activities fairly independently, but do help your child to get started on them if necessary. Remember to discuss each unit and to support your child as much as possible with positive praise as he or she works through the book.

Revision tests

There are three revision tests in the book. The tests assess your child's progress and understanding of the preceding units. They can be marked by either you or your child. Your child should fill in his or her score for each test in the space provided so that a visual record of progress may be kept.

Parents' guide

The parents' guide on pages 6–8 provides you with brief information about each section of the book.

Learner's guide

This gives children some basic ideas about how to approach science learning and revision. It is found on page 9.

Answers

Answers to the pages and revision tests are found on pages 52 to 59.

Glossary

All the words in **bold** are in a glossary on pages 62–63 of this book. These are important words, that your child should know.

Contents

Parents' guide **6**
Learner's guide **9**

Section A	**Keeping healthy**	
Unit 1	Testing diets	**10**
Unit 2	Balanced diets	**11**
Unit 3	Your heart and lungs	**12**
Unit 4	Measuring your pulse rate	**13**
Unit 5	Changing pulse rates	**14**
Unit 6	Drugs and health	**15**

Section B	**Life cycles**	
Unit 7	Fruits and seeds	**16**
Unit 8	Germination	**17**
Unit 9	Parts of a flower	**18**
Unit 10	Plant life cycles	**19**
Unit 11	The human life cycle	**20**
Unit 12	Endangered species	**21**
	Test 1	**22**

Section C	**Gases around us**	
Unit 13	Understanding air	**24**
Unit 14	Powders and sponges	**25**
Unit 15	Air in soil	**26**
Unit 16	Important gases	**27**
Unit 17	Evaporation	**28**
Unit 18	Solids, liquids and gases	**29**

Section D	**Changing state**	
Unit 19	More evaporation	**30**
Unit 20	Investigating evaporation	**31**

Unit 21	Condensation	**32**
Unit 22	Boiling and freezing	**33**
Unit 23	Changes of state	**34**
Unit 24	The water cycle	**35**
	Test 2	**36**

Section E	**Earth, Sun and Moon**	
Unit 25	The Earth, Moon and Sun	**38**
Unit 26	The position of the Sun	**39**
Unit 27	The spinning Earth	**40**
Unit 28	The Sun in winter and summer	**41**
Unit 29	The Earth's orbit	**42**
Unit 30	The Moon's orbit	**43**

Section F	**Changing sounds**	
Unit 31	Vibrations and sound	**44**
Unit 32	Travelling sound	**45**
Unit 33	Stopping sound	**46**
Unit 34	Investigating soundproofing	**47**
Unit 35	Pitch	**48**
Unit 36	Pitch in wind instruments	**49**
	Test 3	**50**

Answers	**52**
Your notes	**60**
Glossary	**62**

Parents' guide

This book is intended to help your child learn and revise the science taught in schools during Year 5. It is the third book in a series of four revision guides that cover the whole of Key Stage 2 science.

The book follows the National Curriculum and a teaching order (called a Scheme of Work) used by the majority of schools in the UK. Children can use this book to revise and reinforce their science work in the same order that it is generally met at school.

The curriculum for science is divided into four main areas:

- Sc1 – 'Scientific enquiry' (the study of how to do experiments)
- Sc2 – 'Life processes and living things' (essentially biology)
- Sc3 – 'Materials and their properties' (essentially chemistry)
- Sc4 – 'Physical processes' (essentially physics)

Sc1

Sc1 is covered throughout this book. The ideas that children meet include how to make predictions and conclusions, and how to draw and interpret bar charts. Fair testing is also covered. Fair testing is a hard concept for children of this age, and your child will need lots of practice. Provide a variety of scenarios to test, and discuss how to make the test fair. The key idea is that only the thing you are actually testing can vary – everything else needs to be kept the same.

Sc2
Section A Keeping healthy

In Year 5, your child will learn about a 'balanced diet'. Encourage him or her to find out more. Can they plan a week's menus, making sure all the food groups are represented?

Your child will also learn about the effects of exercise. Encourage him or her to take more exercise, perhaps substituting a walk to school for a car journey.

In Year 5, children learn about drugs such as nicotine and alcohol, and the dangers of illegal drugs. Make sure you discuss the issues raised. Does your child know the effects of these drugs on the body?

Section B Life cycles

This section teaches your child about the life cycle of plants, including seed dispersal. Look at the ways plants spread their seeds. Ask your child to look at plants with different seeds and describe to you how they are spread.

Germination is also covered. Encourage your child to investigate the process of germination by sprouting beans on damp tissue in a glass jar. Keep the tissue damp, and your child will be able to watch as the root sprouts, and then the shoot grows.

Sunflowers could be grown in a large container. The parts of this plant are easy to observe.

In Year 5, your child also learns about the human life cycle. The key idea that they need to understand is the change in level of independence as a child grows older.

Children will learn about environmental issues, including what it means for animals to be endangered. Encourage your child to find out more about endangered species, and the way in which plants, animals and their habitats may be protected. You can get information from organisations such as the WWF, Plantlife, the Wildlife Trust, the RSPB or the Marine Conservation Society.

Revision test 1
There is a quick test for children to do once they have covered these units. Encourage your child to go back and re-write answers that he or she got wrong.

Sc3
Section C Gases around us
This section is about gases. Encourage your child to physically explore the properties of each state of matter and describe them, concentrating on gases.

Your child could experiment with evaporating puddles. They could draw round a puddle in chalk and observe its size change. Can your child explain what might affect the evaporation process (wind, temperature) and explain where the water has gone?

Section D Changing state
This section is about changing states – melting, freezing, evaporating, condensing. Encourage your child to find examples of condensation. Can they explain how it is created? Show them how to 'mist' a window by breathing on it hard.

Melting and freezing points are met again and boiling points are introduced. It is a common mistake for Year 5 children to think that liquids only evaporate when they boil; make sure your child understands that liquids evaporate *quickest* when boiling.

Revision test 2
There is a quick test for children to do once they have covered these units. Encourage your child to go back and re-write answers that he or she got wrong.

Sc4
Section E Earth, Sun and Moon
Encourage your child to make a model of the Sun, Earth and Moon using a large beach ball for the Sun, a large marble for the Earth and a small pea for the Moon. Can he or she identify each 'ball'?

In Year 5, your child will learn about the movement of the Earth, including the way in which it orbits the Sun. Help your child to understand how the seasons happen.

Observe the way the shadow of a fixed object changes position and size during the course of the day. Can your child explain what is happening in terms of the Earth spinning?

Section F Changing sounds

This section is about sound. Can your child identify a range of sounds, and classify them into loud and soft sounds, and high and low pitch sounds? Can he or she explain in simple terms how we hear sounds?

If you have access to a stringed instrument this will reinforce ideas about how to make sounds higher or lower in pitch and how to make them louder or softer. If you don't have a stringed instrument, a long ruler will do (see page 44).

Revision test 3

There is a quick test for children to do once they have covered these units. Encourage your child to go back and re-write answers that he or she got wrong.

Glossary

All the words in **bold** are in a glossary at the back of the book.

Learner's guide

You can use this book to help you revise the science that you learn at school.

Units

Each page has some things to **remember** and then **have a go** questions.

Read slowly through the information to remember. It often helps to read something and then to close your eyes and see if you can say the information back to yourself. Also, reading things again and again will help you remember things.

It can be a good idea to write down a few words to remind yourself of what you are learning on a page.

When you think you know all the information, then answer the questions. Write down your answers and check to see whether you got them right using pages 52–59.

If you get an answer wrong, go back and make sure you understand why you got it wrong. You can always ask someone like a parent or teacher to help you.

Tests

After every 2 sections there is a test. Write the answers to the test and then check them. If you get an answer wrong, go back and make sure you understand why you got it wrong. You can always ask someone like a parent or teacher to help you.

Your notes

Use pages 60–61 for your own notes. For example, you could write down things you have found difficult so you know which things you should study again. You also write down ways that you have found to remember things.

Glossary

All the words in **bold** in the book are important words and you should learn their meanings. There is a list of these words and their meanings at the back of the book in the glossary section (pages 62–63).

We hope you enjoy using this book, and we wish you every success with your science studies!

Unit 1: Testing diets

● Remember

In Paris in the eighteenth century, doctors were amazed to find that babies from wealthy families were not surviving as well as babies from poorer families.

Wealthy babies were fed bread, butter and boiled milk, and poorer babies were fed potatoes and gravy.

Doctors came up with the idea that something was missing from the wealthy babies' **diet**. To test this idea, they got wealthy babies to be fed potatoes, fresh milk and lemon juice – the same sort of diet as poorer babies. After this, many more wealthy babies survived. Today we know that the wealthy babies became sick because of a lack of **vitamins** in their diet.

● Have a go

1 True or false? Write T or F in the box.

   a Babies from wealthy families in the eighteenth century were healthier than poorer babies.

   b Doctors in eighteenth century Paris knew all about vitamins.

   c The wealthy babies became ill because their diet contained too much bread.

   d Doctors and scientists think up ideas about why things happen and then do experiments to test these ideas.

2 Why were the diets of babies from poorer families healthier than those from richer families?

_____

_____

3 Do you know what a scientific idea is called? Have a guess. Circle one word.

   eureka   invention   theory   vitamin

Unit 2: Balanced diets

Remember

To stay healthy, we need to eat a **balanced diet**, which means eating foods from different **food groups**.

- Foods that contain **proteins** help us grow. Examples are eggs, fish and cheese.
- Foods that contain **carbohydrates** give us energy. Examples are bread and pasta.
- Foods containing **fats** give us a store of energy. Examples are cheese, olive oil and butter.
- Fruit and vegetables give us **vitamins** and **fibre**. Fibre helps keep your insides healthy.
- Water helps us to digest food and to replace water lost from our bodies.

We shouldn't eat too many foods that contain a lot of fat or sugar. These can be bad for us.

Have a go

1. What does the word 'diet' mean? _____

2. What is a balanced diet? _____
   _____

3. Why should we eat plenty of fruit and vegetables? _____
   _____

4. Why should we drink plenty of water? _____
   _____

5. Which two food groups give us energy for activity? _____
   _____

6. What do protein foods help our bodies to do? _____
   _____

Unit 3: Your heart and lungs

Remember

We need exercise to keep our muscles healthy. When we exercise, our muscles work hard, and our lungs and heart work hard too.

Your **heart** and **lungs** are found under your ribs. Your ribs protect the heart and lungs.

Your heart is a pump that pushes the blood around your body to all the places where it is needed – your muscles, brain and lungs for example. The muscle wall of the heart contracts and squeezes the blood inside, forcing the blood to move through the body in tubes called **blood vessels**.

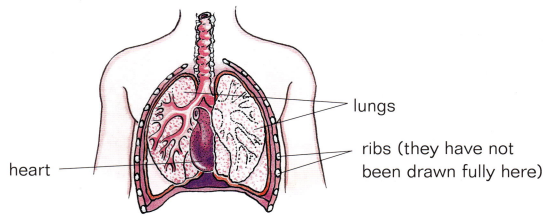

Have a go

1. True or false? Write T or F in the box.

   a The heart and lungs are in the stomach.

   b The heart and lungs are protected by ribs.

   c When you exercise, your muscles work harder.

   d The ribs protect the brain.

   e The heart is a pump.

   f Blood moves around the body in blood tubes.

   g When the heart muscle wall contracts, blood is pushed around the body.

Unit 4: Measuring your pulse rate

🔴 Remember

When your muscles are working hard, your heart works harder to pump the oxygen-rich blood around your body quickly, and this makes your **pulse rate** rise. You can feel your pulse in your neck or wrist.

To measure your pulse rate, count how many times you can feel your pulse beat in one minute. Pulse rates are measured in beats per minute. Your pulse rate changes all the time, so you need to measure it several times to be sure of the rate.

🔴 Have a go

1 True or false? Write T or F in the box.

   a When you exercise, your heart beats more slowly.

   b Your lungs pump blood around your body.

   c You can feel your pulse in your neck or wrist.

2 What does your pulse rate measure? Tick one box.

   ☐ The number of times you breathe in a minute.

   ☐ How many times your heart beats in a minute.

   ☐ How many steps you can take in a minute.

   ☐ How hot you get when exercising.

3 a John counted his pulse 61 times in 1 minute. What is his pulse rate?

   _____

   b Yasmin counted her pulse 16 times in 15 seconds. What is her pulse rate?

   _____

   c What is your own pulse rate? _____

Unit 5: Changing pulse rates

Darren is carrying out an investigation about pulse rates. He has made a prediction.

I think my pulse rate will go up when I start to play tennis because my muscles will be working harder and will need more blood. I think my pulse rate will fall when I stop playing.

Darren measures his pulse rate once before he starts playing tennis, then again after he has just finished, and then again after every 2 minutes. This **line graph** shows his results.

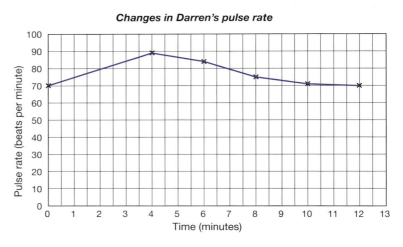

Use the graph to help you to answer the questions.

1 After how many minutes did Darren stop playing tennis?

_____

2 a What happened to his pulse rate after he stopped? _____

b Why did this happen? _____

_____

3 Was Darren's prediction correct? _____

4 What could Darren have done to make his measurements more accurate and so make his investigation better? (*Hint: have a look at the previous page if you're stuck!*) _____

_____

5 What was Darren's pulse rate 8 minutes after his investigation started?

_____

Unit 6: Drugs and health

A **drug** is a substance that affects the way your body works. Tobacco contains a drug called **nicotine**, which makes people feel relaxed. But nicotine is **addictive** and this makes it very hard to give up smoking. Scientists have found that smoking tobacco in cigarettes is the cause of a great many illnesses, including cancer.

Alcohol is also a drug. Some drugs, such as ecstasy and cocaine, are **illegal** and can make people very ill – and can even kill them.

Medicines are also drugs, and can also harm people if they are not taken in the way that is recommended.

In the space below, design a poster telling people how to stay healthy by being sensible about drugs. Include all the words in bold above in your poster.

Unit 7: Fruits and seeds

Remember

Flowering plants produce **fruits** from their flowers. The fruits contain **seeds**, and many of these will grow into new plants.

Seeds need to be spread away from the parent plant to have a better chance of growing into new plants.

Seeds are spread in many ways. They may be spread when animals such as birds eat the fruits. This happens with plants that have seeds inside juicy fruits, such as blackberries and apples. Seeds may also be spread by the wind. This happens when the fruits are in the form of fluffy parachutes or wings, such as dandelions and sycamore trees. Others, such as peas and Himalayan balsam, are spread by explosion – the seeds are flung far from the plant as the fruit (called a pod) pops. Other seeds, such as coconuts, are spread as they float away on water.

Have a go

1. How are the following seeds spread? Choose from explosion, being eaten by animals, and being carried by the wind.

    a Sycamore seeds _____

    b Holly berries _____

    c Raspberries _____

2. How do you think the seeds in fruits A, B and C above are spread?

    A _____

    B _____

    C _____

3. Why do seeds need to be spread? _____

    _____

4. Why don't all seeds grow into new plants? _____

Unit 8: Germination

Have you ever grown plants from seeds? They need warmth and water to start to grow. Seeds bought in packets are sealed with foil to keep them dry and fresh. If they get damp, they may start to sprout!

For green plants to grow healthily, they need light. But seeds do not need light to start to grow. They **germinate** (start to grow) just as well in the dark.

1 a Use the equipment below to design a fair test to show that seeds do not need light to germinate.

water   pots   soil   seeds   dark cupboard   light shelf

Write your plan here.

_____
_____
_____
_____
_____
_____

b Why should you use more than one seed for each part of your investigation? _____

_____
_____

Unit 9: Parts of a flower

Remember

When an organism makes new organisms, it is said to **reproduce**. Plants reproduce by making seeds. The first step in making seeds is **pollination**. This is when **pollen** is carried from the **anther** of one flower to the **stigma** of another flower. The pollen is sometimes blown by the wind, and sometimes carried by insects such as bees.

Different plants produce different types of pollen. Some grains are spiky and sticky (to attach to insects' bodies). Some are very small and light (to float on the wind).

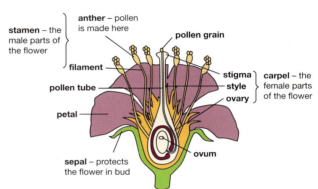

When a grain of pollen reaches the stigma, it grows a tube down to the **ovum**. A part of the pollen grain joins with the ovum. This is called **fertilisation**. The seed can then start to grow (the ovum forms part of it).

Have a go

1. Each sentence contains a mistake. Write out a correct version of each sentence.

   a Pollen grains are made in the stigma. _____

   _____

   b The female parts of the flower are the stigma, style and petal.

   _____

   c Pollination is when the pollen joins with the ovum. _____

   _____

   d Pollen grains that are carried by the wind are large and sticky.

   _____

Unit 10: Plant life cycles

Remember

The stages in a plant's life make up its **life cycle**. Below is the life cycle of an apple tree.

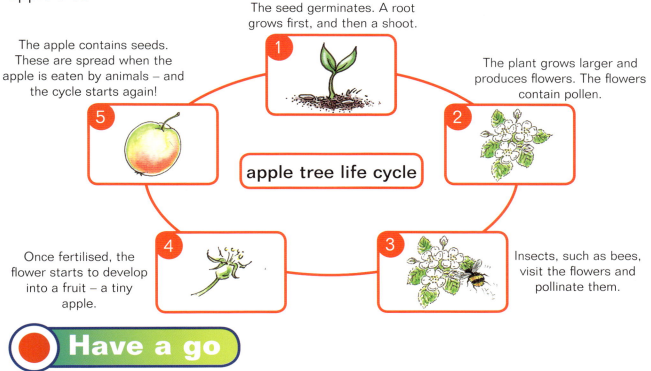

Have a go

Choose a plant, and in the space draw its life cycle with five stages. Write about each stage of the life cycle alongside.

1 _____

2 _____

3 _____

4 _____

5 _____

Unit 11: The human life cycle

Remember

Humans have a life cycle, just like other organisms. When humans are born, they are helpless and depend on their parents to do everything for them. Toddlers are a little more independent, and learn to do things such as eat with a spoon and use the toilet. Children can do more things but still need the care of an adult. Teenagers can do most things that adults can do, and in a few years they become completely grown up and can have children of their own.

Other animals are far less dependent on their parents. For example, foals and calves are able to walk very soon after they are born (although they need milk from their mothers).

Have a go

1. In the spaces below, draw a human life cycle.

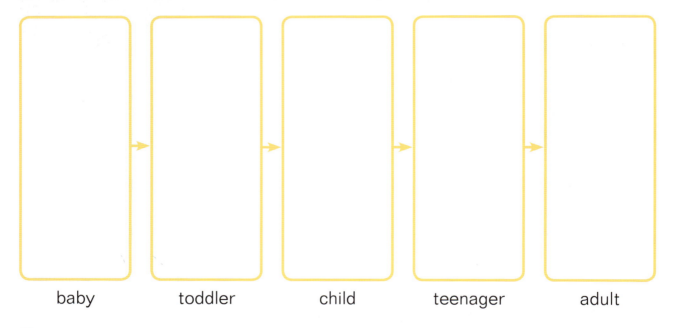

baby   toddler   child   teenager   adult

2. What can a toddler do that a baby can't? _____

_____

_____

3. Which are looked after by their parents for a shorter length of time – human babies or puppies? _____

Unit 12: Endangered species

Remember

When animals have babies, we say they have **reproduced**. That means they have made more creatures, just like them. Plants also reproduce, using seeds. When animals do not have enough babies to replace the ones that die, the animals are said to be **endangered**. This means that there is the danger that the group of animals will die out completely.

Pandas, tigers and cheetahs are all animals whose numbers have fallen. There are laws to stop people killing them, but people called poachers sometimes kill them anyway and sell the fur or other parts for money.

Endangered animals also suffer when people build farms or homes in places where the animals prefer to live.

Many zoos and wildlife parks in the UK try to breed endangered animals in captivity. That means they try to encourage them to have babies in the zoo. Some of these babies may be put back into the animals' natural habitats.

Have a go

1. True or false? Write T or F in the boxes.

   a When animals have babies, we say they have replied.

   b When animals are said to be endangered, it means there are not many of them in the world.

   c Poachers protect animals in the wild.

2. How can plants become endangered? _____

3. Find out the names of three more animals that are endangered.

Test 1

Check how much you have learned.
Answer the questions.
Mark your answers. Fill in your score.

SCORE

① What word means 'what you eat'?

_____

out of 1

② Plan a healthy meal that includes foods for activity, growth and health.

_____

_____

out of 3

③ Why do we need to take exercise?

_____

out of 1

④ What do your ribs do? _____

_____

out of 2

⑤ a The drug in cigarettes is nicotine. What is a drug?

_____

_____

  b What disease can cigarette smoking cause?

_____

out of 2

⑥ a How do coconut seeds spread?

_____

  b How are the seeds inside holly berries spread?

_____

out of 2

⑦ What conditions do seeds need to germinate?

_____

out of 1

8 Draw lines from the labels to the correct parts of the flower.

anther   stigma   ovum   petal   style

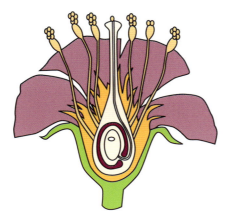

out of 5

9 Look at this line graph.

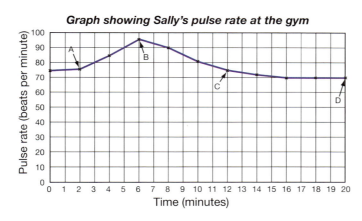

a At which point (A to D) was Sally exercising the hardest?

_____

b What was Sally's pulse rate when she was not exercising?

_____

10 What does 'endangered species' mean?

_____
_____

out of 1

out of 1

out of 1

Total out of 20

Unit 13: Understanding air

Remember

It might seem as though the air is not made of anything, but we can feel it is there every time the wind blows – so it must be made of something.

Everything around us is made of **matter**. Matter can be in three different forms: solid, liquid or **gas**. These are called the three **states of matter**. The air is made of gases.

Everything has a **mass**, which is a measure of how much matter is in it. Masses are measured in **grams (g)** and **kilograms (kg)**. Gases have a lower mass than solids and liquids.

Have a go

1. What would happen to these things if air was not made of anything?

   a _____

   _____

   _____

   _____

   b _____

   _____

   _____

   _____

2. Which of these has the least mass? Circle one.

   gas   liquid   solid

3. What units are used to measure mass? _____

   _____

4. Name one thing that is made of gases. _____

   _____

Unit 14: Powders and sponges

Remember

In an investigation, the things you see happening are your **observations**. In one investigation, a sponge was held underwater and squeezed. Bubbles came out of it.

You need to explain your observations. The explanation for the bubbles when the sponge was squeezed is that there are gaps in the solid sponge that are filled with air. When the sponge is squeezed, the air is squashed out and forms bubbles.

It is often a good idea to repeat making observations in an investigation, so that you are sure that your observations are correct.

Have a go

1. Mohammed pours some water into a jar of marbles. He notices bubbles coming up.

    a   What are Mohammed's observations? _____

    _____

    b   How could Mohammed explain these observations? _____

    _____

    c   How could he make sure his observations were correct? _____

    _____

2. a   What do you predict would happen if you poured water into some dry sand until it covered the sand? _____

    _____

    b   Why do you think this will happen? _____

    _____

Unit 15: Air in soil

● Remember

Soil has air in it. This is useful because many animals that live underground need air, just like we do. However, some soils contain more air than others.

Class 5C did an investigation to find out how much air was in three different soils. The children took 200 g of dry soil and put it in a jar. Then they filled a measuring cylinder with 100 cm³ of water, and added the water to the soil until no more would soak into it. They worked out how much water they had added by subtracting the amount left in the measuring cylinder from 100 cm³.

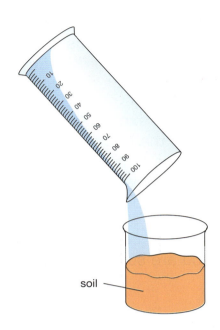

They did this with three different soils.

● Have a go

1 a Complete the table of results.

soil	amount of water left in measuring cylinder (cm³)	amount of water soaked up by soil (cm³)
A	60	
B	40	
C	65	

  b Which soil soaked up the most water? _____

  c Which soil had the most air in it? _____

2 How would Class 5C check that these results were correct?

_____

_____

3 What would they keep the same to make this a fair test?

_____

_____

Unit 16: Important gases

Remember

The air is made of many different gases, including:

- **oxygen** (needed by our bodies)
- **nitrogen** (used to fill crisp packets to stop crisps going stale)
- **carbon dioxide** (used to make some drinks fizzy).

There are many other gases too. We use **helium** to make balloons rise in the air. We use **natural gas** to cook with.

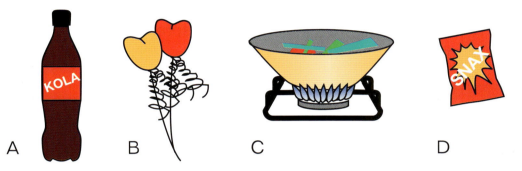

A   B   C   D

Have a go

1. What gas is used in each of A–D?

    a The gas used in A is _____

    b The gas used in B is _____

    c The gas used in C is _____

    d The gas used in D is _____

2. A man is very ill in hospital. What gas might he be given to help him breathe? _____

3. Name three gases found in the air.

    _____

4. Find out the name of another gas and what it is used for.

    _____

    _____

Unit 17: Evaporation

Remember

Gases are formed when liquids **evaporate**. Think of a puddle of rain that dries in the sunlight. It disappears because the liquid has been heated, and has changed into a gas. It is evaporation that makes washing dry when it is hung on the line. When a kettle boils, water changes quickly from a liquid to a gas. The gas is called steam or **water vapour**.

Gases can flow easily from place to place. If you put a dish of perfume on the table and walk across the room, you can still smell it. We smell things when gases enter our noses. The perfume evaporates from the dish and makes a gas which spreads through the air and we smell it.

Have a go

1. What is the gas called that is made when water is heated?

   _____

2. What do we call the process that dries washing hung on the line? _____

   _____

3. What happens to the water when a kettle is boiled? _____

   _____

4. How do we smell things like perfume? _____

   _____

   _____

   _____

5. The natural gas we use to cook with can cause explosions if it leaks. Natural gas has a smell added to it before reaching our homes. Why?

   _____

   _____

   _____

Unit 18: Solids, liquids and gases

Remember

Solids, liquids and gases have different **properties**. **Solids** keep their shape and volume, and do not flow. **Liquids** flow and take on the shape of the container you put them in, but they keep their volume. **Gases** flow even more easily than liquids, in all directions. Gases spread out to fill their container – think of the way you can smell perfume in a room. Gases can also be squashed – think of a bicycle pump.

Have a go

1. The answer to these questions is one or more of: solid, liquid, gas.

   a Which keeps its shape?

   _____

   b Which states of matter take on the shape of their container?

   _____

   c Which flows most easily?

   _____

   d Which flows in all directions?

   _____

2. Describe the properties of a gas. _____

   _____

   _____

3. Give four examples of gases.

   _____

   _____

   _____

   _____

Unit 19: More evaporation

Remember

Gases are made when liquids **evaporate**. **Water vapour** or steam is a gas that is made when water evaporates. Evaporation dries washing when it is hung on the line. The water in puddles evaporates. Water in a kettle also evaporates. When you use a hairdryer, it is evaporation that dries your hair.

All liquids can evaporate. You can smell the gas that evaporates from some liquids, such as perfume.

Have a go

1. What is water vapour (steam)?

   _____

2. What does 'evaporate' mean?

   _____

3. Name two examples of evaporation.

   _____

   _____

4. How does a hairdryer dry your hair?

   _____

5. Name a liquid you can smell when it evaporates.

   _____

Unit 20: Investigating evaporation

Remember

Different groups in Class 5D investigated different **factors** that could affect how quickly water evaporates. (A factor is the thing that you change in an investigation.) The bar charts show the results.

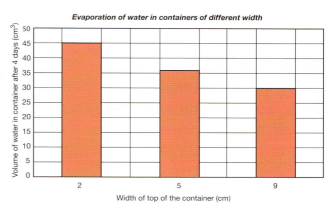

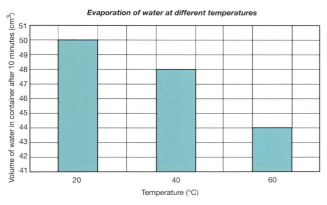

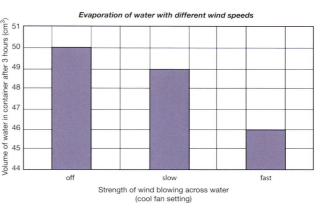

Have a go

1 What factors were investigated?

_____

2 The conclusion for the experiment with temperature is: the higher the temperature, the more the water evaporates. Write conclusions for the other two experiments.

_____

_____

_____

3 a Which of these hairdryer settings do you think will dry hair fastest? Tick one.

☐ low heat, slow fan   ☐ high heat, slow fan

☐ low heat, fast fan   ☐ high heat, fast fan

b Explain why you made this choice. _____

_____

Unit 21: Condensation

Remember

Imagine you are making a cup of tea. It is very cold outside. As the kettle boils, some of the water evaporates into the kitchen. As the water vapour in the air hits the cold windows, it cools down suddenly and water droplets form on the windows. When a gas turns into a liquid it is called **condensation**.

Sometimes you can see condensation on a cold bathroom mirror as the hot tap is running and the bathroom fills with steam. On hot days, we are less likely to see condensation on windows because the outside surface of the glass will not be cold.

Have a go

1. True or false? Write T or F in the box.

   a Condensation appears on windows when it is hot outside.

   b When water vapour hits a cold surface, it condenses.

   c Condensation occurs when steam hits a cold surface.

   d Condensation is the opposite of evaporation.

2. Many people think the white cloud coming from a kettle is steam. It's not! It is condensed steam. Steam or water vapour cannot be seen. Draw lines from the labels to the points on this kettle.

Water vapour (steam) leaves the kettle.

The water vapour condenses in the cooler air and you can see it.

Water is evaporating.

Unit 22: Boiling and freezing

Remember

The **freezing point** of water is zero degrees Celsius (0 °C). Its **melting point** is also 0 °C. At exactly 0 °C the water is freezing, but the ice is melting at the same time. Below 0 °C all the water becomes ice, and above 0 °C all the ice becomes water.

The **boiling point** of water is 100 °C. At this temperature the water is evaporating as fast as it can. Liquid water cannot get hotter than 100 °C (although steam can).

Have a go

1 a What temperature is the freezing point of water? _____

    b The freezing point of some lava (melted rock) in a volcano is 1000 °C. What temperature is the melting point of rock?

_____

    c The melting point of iron is 1535 °C. What is its freezing point?

_____

    d Do you think the boiling point of iron is above or below 1535 °C?

_____

2 Some ice cubes are left in a room at 20 °C.

    a What will the ice look like after 24 hours? _____

    b What temperature will it be? Circle one.

                 0 °C   10 °C   20 °C   24 °C   100 °C

3 What is the hottest temperature that liquid water can be?

_____

Unit 23: Changes of state

● Remember

When something melts, freezes, evaporates or condenses, we say that it 'changes state'. Water vapour is made when water evaporates and changes from a liquid to a gas. When there is a lot of water vapour in the air, some of it condenses on cold surfaces to form tiny droplets of liquid.

Condensing is the opposite of evaporating. When we evaporate a liquid, it is easy to turn the gas back into a liquid. Evaporation is a **reversible change**.

When a solid melts, this is also a reversible change. Freezing is also reversible.

● Have a go

1 True or false? Write T or F in the box.

   a   When steam hits a hot surface, it condenses.

   b   When a window 'steams up', it is because of condensation.

   c   When we boil a pan of water, some of the water evaporates into the air.

   d   Condensation is not a reversible change.

   e   When candle wax melts, it changes state.

2 Add words to this diagram to show the changes of state. Two words have been added for you.

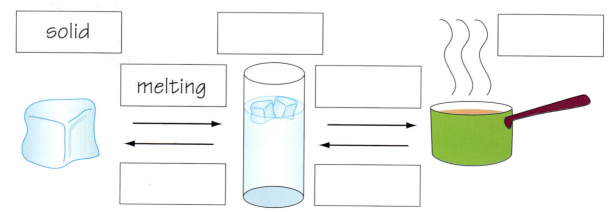

34

Unit 24: The water cycle

Remember

Water from lakes, rivers and seas evaporates into the air. Later it falls as rain, and the whole cycle starts again. This is called the **water cycle**.

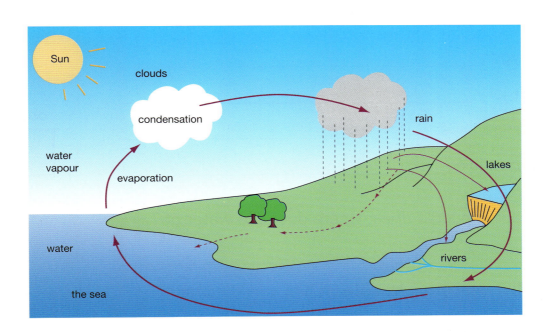

Have a go

1. Here is a children's story about what happens to Derek the drip. Complete the story by filling in the missing words. Use the words on the diagram above to help you.

   Derek the drip enjoyed life in the sea. Until one day the _____ warmed up the seawater so much that Derek _____ and turned into a gas called _____ _____. Derek found this a very strange experience as he floated higher and higher above the _____. As he got higher he got colder, until he _____ and Derek the drip turned back into a drop. *That's better*, thought Derek. After a while the drip found himself dropping back towards the ground as _____. He ended up in a fast-flowing _____ and soon he was back in the sea.

Test 2

Check how much you have learned.

Answer the questions.
Mark your answers. Fill in your score.

SCORE

1 Solid, liquid or gas?

  a oxygen _____

  b set jelly _____

  c orange juice _____

  d frozen juice _____

out of 2

2 a When a puddle dries, where does the water go?

  _____

  b What happens when steam hits a cold surface?

  _____

out of 2

3 a What temperature is the freezing point of water?

  _____

  b An ice cube was left to melt in a room where the temperature was 21 degrees Celsius. What would the temperature of the water be after 36 hours?

  _____

out of 2

1 a The freezing point of paraffin wax is 48 °C. What is its melting point?

  _____

  _____

  b In what state of matter is paraffin wax at room temperature? _____

  _____

out of 2

5. In an investigation, water was poured into a jar of soil. Bubbles came out of the soil and the amount of water that soaked into the soil was measured.

   a What was the observation?

   _____

   b What were the bubbles made of?

   _____

   c Why is it useful that soil has this substance in it?

   _____

   out of 3

6. Rock can be turned into lava by melting it. The melted rock can be made back into a solid again. Fill in the missing words in the sentences.

   a When melted rock turns into a solid, the process is called _____

   b This is a change of _____

   c Since you can melt the rock again, this is a _____ change.

   out of 3

7. Draw lines to match the temperatures with their correct values.

   room temperature   about 20 °C

   freezing point of water   100 °C

   boiling point of water   0 °C

   out of 3

8. Write down three properties of gases.

   _____

   _____

   _____

   out of 3

   Total out of 20

Unit 25: The Earth, Moon and Sun

Remember

The Earth is a sphere, like a ball, but it is only in the past 40 years that we have been able to see this from space. Other forms of evidence (such as ships being able to sail around the world) were needed to show that the Earth is a sphere.

If you made a model of the Sun, the Moon and the Earth, the Sun would be the biggest sphere, the Earth would be a very much smaller sphere and the Moon would be smaller still.

	distance from Earth (kilometres)	distance across or diameter (kilometres)
Earth	0	13 000
Moon	380 000	3500
Sun	150 000 000	1 400 000

When we look at the Sun and the Moon in the sky, they seem to be the same size. This is because the Sun, although much bigger, is much further away from the Earth. You must never look directly at the Sun as this can damage your eyes.

Have a go

1 a About 300 years ago, some people still thought the world was flat. What would you say to them to convince them that it is a sphere?

_____

_____

_____

b What evidence do we have today that shows that the Earth is a sphere?

_____

_____

_____

Unit 26: The position of the Sun

Remember

At midday when the Sun is directly overhead, shadows are short and fat. Shadows are longer in the early morning and late afternoon, when the Sun is low in the sky.

The Sun seems to rise up and move across the sky during the day. There are two possible reasons for this. Either the Sun is moving around the Earth, or the Earth is spinning and the Sun stays where it is. Today we know that the second reason is true.

Have a go

1. Why does the Sun seem to move across the sky during the course of the day? _____

   _____

2. When is the Sun directly overhead? _____

3. Are shadows longer in the morning or at midday? _____

4. Draw how the cat's shadow would look:

a   midday

b   late afternoon

Unit 27: The spinning Earth

Remember

The Earth spins on its **axis** and this is what makes it seem as if the Sun moves across the sky. The axis is like an invisible line running through the centre of the Earth from pole to pole. The Earth spins around once every 24 hours. It is daytime on the part of the Earth that faces the Sun, and night on the part of the Earth facing away from the Sun.

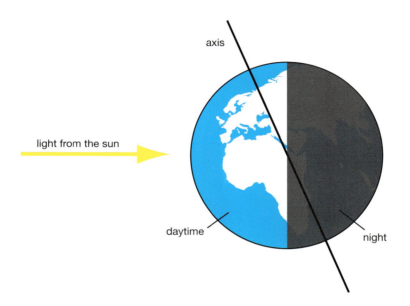

Have a go

1. Which time of the day is it when the part of the Earth you are standing on is facing away from the Sun?

   _____

2. Which time of the day is it when the part of the Earth you are standing on is facing towards the Sun?

   _____

3. What is the 'axis' of the Earth? _____

   _____

4. How long does it take for the Earth to turn once on its axis?

   _____

Unit 28: The Sun in winter and summer

 **Remember**

Each day, the Sun appears to rise in the east and to set in the west. But it does not rise and set in exactly the same place each day, or rise and set at the same time.

The **line graph** shows the times for sunrise and sunset in Cardiff in Wales during a year.

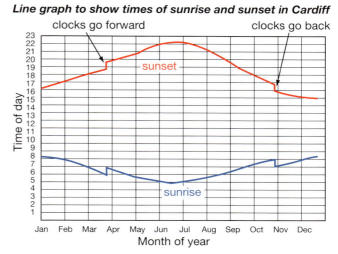

 **Have a go**

1 What happens to the time of sunset in the first 6 months of the year?

_____

2 In September, as the time of sunrise gets later, what happens to the time of sunset? _____

3 a In which month do we get most hours of daylight?

_____

b To the nearest hour, what is the highest number of daylight hours we get in a day? _____

_____

c At what time is sunrise when we get this number of hours of daylight?

_____

4 Which direction does the Sun rise from in the morning?

_____

Unit 29: The Earth's orbit

Remember

The Earth orbits the Sun, spinning as it goes. **Orbit** means moving in a circle around something at the centre of the circle. Think of a group of people with a person running in a circle around them. The group of people is like the Sun, and the person running around it is like the Earth.

It takes the Earth one year to make one complete orbit of the Sun. At different places in the orbit, the Sun rises and sets at different times of the day. This helps to produce the seasons. In summer the days are longer and the Earth is warmed more by the Sun.

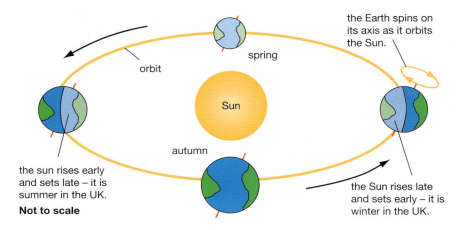

Have a go

1 Choose the correct words from the boxes below to complete the sentences.

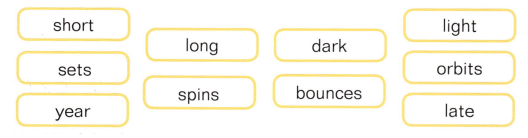

a In the summer, the evenings are _____ and light.

b In winter, it gets _____ earlier.

c The Earth _____ as it goes around the Sun.

d The Earth _____ the Sun.

e It takes one _____ for the Earth to orbit the Sun.

Unit 30: The Moon's orbit

Remember

Evidence is any observation or measurement that is used to show that a scientific idea (**theory**) is correct. Scientists know that the Moon orbits the Earth once every 28 days. So what is the evidence for this?

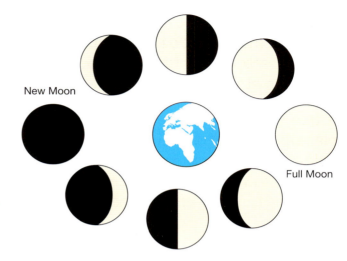

Recent evidence comes from space, where space probes can see that the Moon goes around the Earth. Other evidence includes the observation that the Moon seems to change shape over the course of 28 days. Of course, it doesn't actually change shape – we just see different amounts of the sunlit side of the Moon. It takes 28 days to go from one full Moon to the next.

Have a go

1 Draw lines to match each event with the correct number.

years for Earth to orbit the Sun	1
days for the Moon to orbit the Earth	24
hours for the Earth to turn once	28

2 How much of the sunlit side of the Moon can you see when it is full?

_____

3 Rewrite this sentence to have the same meaning, but without using the underlined word.

The Moon <u>orbits</u> the Earth.

_____

Unit 31: Vibrations and sound

● Remember

If you flick a ruler, it makes a sound as it wobbles up and down (or **vibrates**). When it stops vibrating, it stops making a sound.

When something vibrates, it makes a sound. But how do you hear it? The sound travels through the air and into your ears. Your ears and brain work together to allow you to hear the sound.

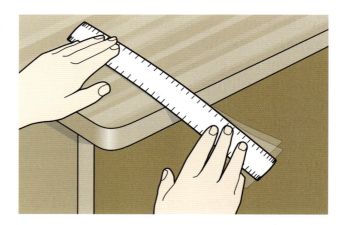

● Have a go

1 a Put two fingers on the front of your neck. Now make a humming noise. What did you feel? _____
_____

b This feeling is caused by the vocal cords in your throat doing something. What are they doing?
_____
_____

2 a Some dry rice is put on the top of a drum, and the drum is hit. What do you think you will see happening to the rice? Make a prediction.
_____
_____

b Why do you think this will happen? _____
_____

3 What does sound travel into that lets you hear it? _____

Unit 32: Travelling sound

● Remember

We know that sound travels through air because that's how sound normally reaches our ears. But does sound travel through solids and liquids?

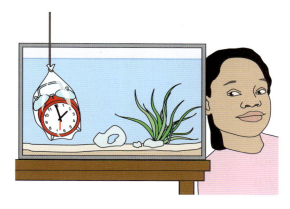

Becky did an investigation to find out. She put a ticking clock in a sealed plastic bag. She sat 1 metre away from the clock and could hear it. She then put the clock on a wooden surface and pressed her ear to the surface. The clock sounded much louder. She then put the clock into a fish tank full of water and placed her ear to the opposite end of the tank, 1 metre away. The clock was louder than in air, but less loud than through the wooden surface.

● Have a go

1 What was Becky trying to find out? What was her **aim**? _____

_____

2 Complete this table to show Becky's results.

what state of matter the sound travelled through	loudness
solid	

3 How far away from the clock on the wooden surface should she put her ear, to make this a fair test? _____

4 a Do sounds travel through solids and liquids? _____

   b Which state of matter do sounds travel through best? _____

   c How do you know this? _____

_____

_____

Unit 33: Stopping sound

Remember

Sometimes we want to stop sounds from travelling. Some people are disturbed in their sleep by sounds and so they wear earplugs to stop the sounds entering their ears. Some people use very noisy machinery in their work and so wear ear protectors to stop too much sound getting into their ears. If sounds are too loud, they can damage your hearing.

Have a go

1. Find two places in your house that have different coverings on the floor (e.g. carpet, tiles, floorboards). Wearing shoes, walk across each floor, listening carefully.

   a On which floor were your footsteps louder? _____

   b Which floor covering is better at stopping sounds from travelling?
   _____

2. a Why do people who direct aeroplanes on the ground at airports wear ear protectors? _____
   _____

   b Think of another place where people would need to wear ear protectors.
   _____

3. Why do some people wear earplugs at night? _____
   _____

Unit 34: Investigating soundproofing

Class 5F investigated which materials are best at **soundproofing** (stopping sounds from travelling). They took a buzzer and put it in a box, which they covered with a single layer of material. They then went into the school hall and found out how far away the box had to be before they could no longer hear it.

The bar chart shows their results.

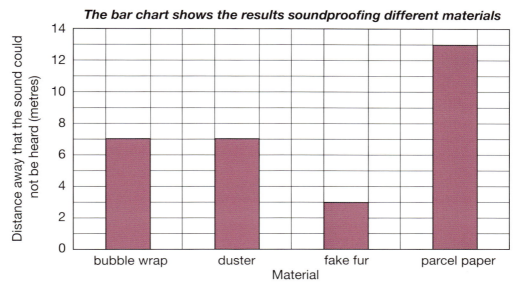

① What things would need to be kept the same to make this a fair test?

_____

_____

② How far away did members of Class 5F have to be before they could no longer hear the buzzer when it was wrapped in the duster?

_____

③ a Which was the best soundproofing material? _____

   b How can you tell? _____

   _____

④ Predict which of these materials is the best at soundproofing. Circle one.

   carpet   kitchen foil   plastic bag   wrapping paper

Unit 35: Pitch

Remember

If you hit a drum lightly, it makes a soft sound. If you hit it hard, it's loud.

Sounds can also be high or low, and this is called **pitch**. A large drum makes a low-pitched sound and a small drum makes a high-pitched sound. This is because of the amount of material that is vibrating. When a large amount of material vibrates, it makes a lower sound than a small amount of material vibrating. The larger drum has more material to vibrate.

It's the same for stringed instruments. Thicker strings make sounds with lower pitches than thinner ones. Longer strings make lower-pitched sounds than shorter ones. You can make the length of a string that vibrates shorter by putting your finger on it.

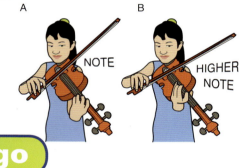

Have a go

1. Put a ruler on the edge of a table, as shown on page 44. Flick the ruler and listen to the sound. Now project less of the ruler over the edge, and flick it again.

    a   Was the sound higher or lower than when you first flicked the ruler?
    _____

    b   Why was this? _____
    _____

2. How is the violinist playing a higher note in picture B?
    _____
    _____

3. Which of these words describe high sounds? Circle them.

    boom   clank   ding   dong   screech
    squeak   thud   thump   ting

Unit 36: Pitch in wind instruments

● Remember

When you play a recorder, the air inside it starts to vibrate, and this vibrating air produces a note. If you have all the holes on the recorder covered by your fingers, you play the lowest note on the instrument. If you lift up some fingers, the note becomes higher. This is because you have made the length of air vibrating inside the instrument shorter. If there is less of something vibrating, the note is higher.

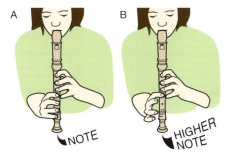

● Have a go

1 Use the clues to complete the crossword.

Across
1. Sounds travel best through this state of matter.
3. How high or low a sound is.
5. Materials that are good at stopping sounds are said to be good at _____.
6. When a drum makes a sound it does this.

Down
2. A drum that is hit harder makes a _____ sound.
3. People who operate noisy machinery wear ear _____.
4. A short flicked ruler makes a _____ sound than a long one.
5. The things that vibrate on a guitar.
7. The thing that vibrates inside a recorder.
8. You hear sounds when they travel into your _____.

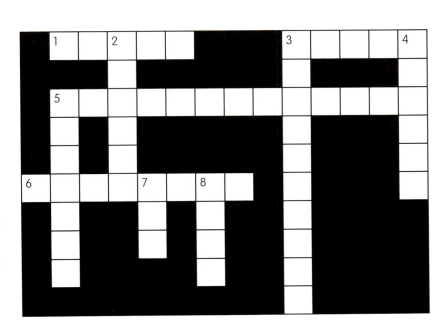

Test 3

Check how much you have learned.

Answer the questions.
Mark your answers. Fill in your score.

SCORE

1 a The Earth turns around an imaginary line. What is this line called? _____

   b How long does one turn take? _____

out of 2

2 Complete these sentences by circling the correct words.

   a We get the most daily hours of sunlight in spring/summer/autumn/winter.

   b The Sun appears to rise in the east/west/north/south.

out of 2

3 Rewrite these sentences, correcting the mistakes.

   a The Earth takes 1 month to orbit the Sun.

   _____

   b The Moon takes 28 days to orbit the Sun.

   _____

   c The whole Earth has daytime at the same time.

   _____

out of 3

4 a Put these in order of size (smallest first): the Sun, the Moon and the Earth.

   _____ _____ _____

   b Why does the Sun look the same size as the Moon from the Earth?

   _____

out of 3

5 What must something do to make a sound?

   _____

out of 1

50

6 Draw how the girl's shadow would look:

a at midday

b in the late afternoon

out of 2

7 a You play a note on a guitar. Write down two ways in which you could play a higher-pitched note.

_____

_____

b How could you play a louder note?

_____

out of 3

out of 1

8 What sort of materials are best at soundproofing?

_____

out of 1

9 When might a person have to wear ear protectors?

_____

out of 1

10 Which will sound travel through best? Circle one.

water   wood   milk   air   perfume

out of 1

11 What do we use to hear sounds? _____

Total out of 20

Answers

Unit 1: Testing diets (page 10)

1.
   a F
   b F
   c F
   d T

2. The diets of poorer babies contained more vitamins.

3. theory

Unit 2: Balanced diets (page 11)

1. What you eat.

2. Eating a wide variety of foods from different food groups.

3. They contain lots of vitamins and fibre.

4. It helps us digest food and replaces water lost from our bodies.

5. carbohydrates and fats

6. They help us grow.

Unit 3: Your heart and lungs (page 12)

1.
   a F
   b T
   c T
   d F
   e T
   f F
   g T

Unit 4: Measuring your pulse rate (page 13)

1.
   a F
   b F
   c T

2. How many times your heart beats in a minute.

3.
   a 61 beats per minute
   b 64 beats per minute (16 × 4 because there are four lots of 15 seconds in 1 minute)
   c Your own answer, which is probably between 65 and 80 beats per minute.

Unit 5: Changing pulse rates (page 14)

1. 4 minutes

2.
   a It fell.
   b His heart started to beat more slowly (because his muscles were working less hard).

3. yes

4. He could have repeated his experiment to make sure he got similar results.

5. 75 beats per minute

Unit 6: Drugs and health (page 15)

Your own poster design, which may include mention of alcohol making you ill, smoking causing serious diseases, illegal drugs being very dangerous, and medicines being dangerous if you don't take them according to the instructions.

Unit 7: Fruits and seeds (page 16)

1.
   a carried by the wind
   b eaten by animals
   c eaten by animals

2. A, eaten by animals; B, spread by the wind; C, spread by the wind

3. To have a better chance of growing into new plants.

4 Any of these reasons: some may be bad seeds, some seeds are eaten by animals, some seeds land in the wrong place and can't grow.

Unit 8: Germination (page 17)

1 a Plant the same number of seeds in the same amount of soil in two pots that are the same. Water both with the same amount of water. Put one in the dark cupboard and the other on the light shelf. Make sure they are at the same temperature. The only thing that should be different is that one is in the dark and the other is in the light.

b To be sure all seeds behave in the same way, or because some seeds might be bad and so won't grow.

Unit 9: Parts of a flower (page 18)

1 a Pollen grains are made in the anther.
b The female parts of the flower are the stigma, style and ovary.
c Pollination is when pollen travels from an anther of one flower to the stigma of another; *or* fertilisation is when the pollen joins with the ovum.
d Pollen grains that are carried by the wind are small and light; *or* pollen grains that are carried by insects are large and sticky.

Unit 10: Plant life cycles (page 19)

A drawing with notes similar to the drawings of the apple tree life cycle on page 19.

Unit 11: The human life cycle (page 20)

1 Drawings of a person at different ages.

2 Feed him/herself and use the toilet.

3 puppies

Unit 12: Endangered species (page 21)

1 a F
b T
c F

2 Reasons such as: people picking/ chopping down too many of them, building homes or farms in the places where the plants like to live, being poisoned by pollution or weedkillers.

3 Any three endangered animals, including many whales, bats and birds of prey.

Test 1

1 diet

2 A meal with food(s) from the carbohydrate group, such as bread or pasta for activity; food(s) from the protein group, such as meat or nuts for growth; small amount(s) of food(s) from the fat group, such as cheese for a store of energy; and fruit and vegetables for fibre and vitamins (score 1 mark for each food group up to a maximum of 3).

3 To keep our muscles healthy.

4 Protect the heart and lungs (score 1 mark for each organ).

5 a A substance that alters how your body or brain behaves.
   b Any one of: cancer, bronchitis, emphysema, heart disease.

6 a by water
   b by being eaten by animals/birds

7 warmth and water $\frac{1}{2}$ mark for each, and take off $\frac{1}{2}$ mark for writing 'light')

8
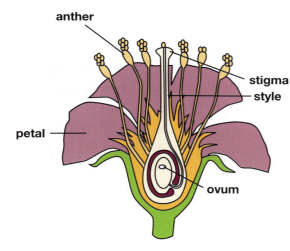

9 a B
   b 70 beats per minute

10 A group of organisms whose numbers are falling.

Unit 13: Understanding air (page 24)

1 a The kite would not fly.
   b The boat would not move.

2 gas

3 grams and kilograms

4 air

Unit 14: Powders and sponges (page 25)

1 a Seeing bubbles coming up.
   b There was air between the marbles that is pushed out by the water.
   c By doing his experiment again.

2 a Bubbles would appear, *or* the water would soak into the sand.
   b There is air between the sand particles that is pushed out by the water.

Unit 15: Air in soil (page 26)

1 a

soil	amount of water left in measuring cylinder (cm³)	amount of water soaked up by soil (cm³)
A	60	40
B	40	60
C	65	35

   b soil B
   c soil B

2 By doing the experiment again.

3 They would use the same container for the soil; and pour in the water in the same way each time.

Unit 16: Important gases (page 27)

1 A, carbon dioxide; B, helium; C, natural gas; D, nitrogen

2 oxygen

3 oxygen, nitrogen, carbon dioxide

(there are others, including, for example, argon)

④ Argon is used in light bulbs, neon is used in coloured light tubes, hydrogen is used in rockets and some car engines. These are only a few examples!

Unit 17: Evaporation (page 28)

① water vapour or steam

② evaporation

③ It changes quickly into water vapour or steam; *or* it evaporates quickly.

④ The liquid perfume evaporates and the gas with the smell spreads through the air into our noses.

⑤ So we can smell it and report gas leaks.

Unit 18: Solids, liquids and gases (page 29)

① a solid
   b liquid, gas
   c gas
   d gas

② can change its shape, can change its volume, flows easily

③ Any four gases, for example: oxygen, carbon dioxide, nitrogen, argon, hydrogen, helium.

Unit 19: More evaporation (page 30)

① Water as a gas.

② Turning from a liquid into a gas.

③ Any two examples of evaporation, for example: puddles drying up, perfume being smelt, washing drying on the line.

④ The hot air from the hairdryer evaporates the water in your hair.

⑤ Any liquid that you can smell when it evaporates, for example: perfume, aftershave, petrol.

Unit 20: Investigating evaporation (page 31)

① The width of the container, the temperature and different wind speeds.

② The wider the top of the container, the more the water evaporates. The stronger the wind, the more the water evaporates.

③ a high heat, fast fan
   b Both increasing heat and wind speed increase water evaporation.

Unit 21: Condensation (page 32)

① a F
   b T
   c T
   d T

②

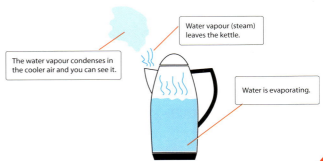

Water vapour (steam) leaves the kettle.

The water vapour condenses in the cooler air and you can see it.

Water is evaporating.

55

Unit 22: Boiling and freezing (page 33)

1.
   a 0 °C
   b 1000 °C
   c 1535 °C
   d above 1535 °C (a material's boiling point is always above its melting point – in fact the boiling point of iron is 2750 °C)

2.
   a liquid water
   b 20 °C

3. 100 °C

Unit 23: Changes of state (page 34)

1.
   a F
   b T
   c T
   d F
   e T

2.

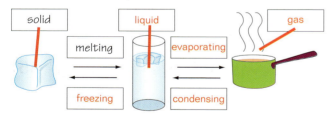

Unit 24: The water cycle (page 35)

1. Sun, evaporated, water vapour, sea/ground, condensed, rain, river

Test 2

1.
   a gas
   b solid
   c liquid
   d solid (score ½ mark for each)

2.
   a into the air, *or* it evaporates, *or* it changes into a gas
   b it condenses, *or* it turns back into a liquid

3.
   a 0 °C
   b 21 °C

4.
   a 48 °C
   b solid

5.
   a bubbles
   b air
   c So that animals that live underground can breathe.

6.
   a freezing
   b state
   c reversible

7. room temperature, about 20 °C; freezing point of water, 0 °C; boiling point of water, 100 °C

8. flow easily, change shape easily, change volume easily

Unit 25: The Earth, Moon and Sun (page 38)

1.
   a Ships can sail around the world.
   b We can see the Earth from space.

Unit 26: The position of the Sun (page 39)

1. because the Earth is spinning
2. at midday/noon
3. morning

4

a midday

b late afternoon

Unit 27: The spinning Earth (page 40)

① night

② day

③ An imaginary line that runs through the centre of the Earth from pole to pole.

④ 24 hours/1 day

Unit 28: The Sun in winter and summer (page 41)

① It gets later and later.

② It gets earlier.

③ a June
   b 17 hours (the difference between the top and bottom lines on the graph in June)
   c 5 a.m.

④ east

Unit 29: The Earth's orbit (page 42)

① a long
   b dark
   c spins
   d orbits
   e year

Unit 30: The Moon's orbit (page 43)

① Years for Earth to orbit the Sun = 1; days for the Moon to orbit the Earth = 28; hours for the Earth to turn once = 24

② All of the sunlit side.

③ The Moon goes around the Earth.

Unit 31: Vibrations and sound (page 44)

① a vibrations in your neck
   b vibrating

② a The rice will bounce.
   b The drum skin vibrates.

③ your ears

Unit 32: Travelling sound (page 45)

① To find out if sound travels through liquids and solids.

②

what state of matter the sound travelled through	loudness
solid	very loud
liquid	loud
gas	not so loud

57

3 1 metre

4 a yes
   b solid
   c The sound was loudest when she listened to the sound of the clock through the solid wooden surface.

Unit 33: Stopping sound (page 46)

1 a On the hard floor.
   b The soft floor.

2 a The sound of aeroplane engines is very loud and could damage their hearing.
   b Examples include: using noisy machinery such as a road drill; working in a noisy factory; on a game show to stop people hearing other people's answers.

3 So they can sleep if there's noise outside or someone snoring.

Unit 34: Investigating soundproofing (page 47)

1 The buzzer, the box the buzzer is in, the person or people doing the listening, the room.

2 7 metres

3 a fake fur
   b It was the material that was the most difficult to hear the buzzer through.

4 carpet

Unit 35: Pitch (page 48)

1 a higher
   b There was less material vibrating.

2 She has shortened the length of string that can vibrate (by putting her finger further up it).

3 ding, screech, squeak, ting

Unit 36: Pitch in wind instruments (page 49)

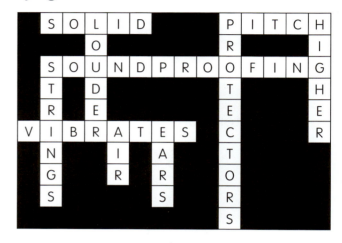

Test 3

1 a axis
   b 24 hours *or* 1 day

2 a We get the most daily hours of sunlight in summer.
   b The Sun appears to rise in the east.

3 a The Earth takes 1 year to orbit the Sun.
   b The Moon takes 28 days to orbit the Earth.
   c Half of the Earth has daytime, while the other half has night.

4 a Moon, Earth, Sun (1 mark for getting Earth bigger than Moon. 1 mark for getting the Sun bigger than Earth).
   b The Moon is much closer to the Earth than the Sun.

58

5 vibrate

6

7 a Two from: make the amount of string that vibrates shorter by putting your finger on some of it, playing one of the thinner strings, tightening the tuning peg to stretch the string and make it thinner (score 1 mark for each up to a maximum of 2)
b Pluck the string harder.

8 soft ones

9 if they are near noisy machinery

10 wood

11 our ears

Your notes

Glossary

addictive Something that is hard to stop doing.

aim What you are trying to find out in an investigation.

anther Part of a flower that makes pollen.

axis An imaginary line that runs through the Earth from pole to pole.

balanced diet Eating a variety of foods from all the different food groups.

blood vessels Tubes that carry blood around your body.

boiling When a liquid is as hot as it can get and is evaporating as fast as it can.

boiling point The temperature at which a liquid is as hot as it can get.

carbohydrate Substance in some foods that gives you energy for activity.

carbon dioxide A gas in the air, used to make fizzy drinks.

carpel Female parts of a flower – stigma, style, ovary.

condensation Turning from a gas into a liquid.

diet What you eat.

drug Substance that affects the way your body works.

endangered If an organism is endangered, there are very few of them left. There is a danger that there will be none of them left in the future.

evaporation Turning from a liquid into a gas.

evidence Any observation or measurement that is used to show that a scientific idea (theory) is correct.

factor The thing that you change in an investigation.

fat Substance in some foods that you need to give you a store of energy. You shouldn't eat too many fatty foods.

fertilisation When part of a pollen grain joins with the ovum in plant reproduction.

fibre Substance found in fruits and vegetables that helps keep your insides healthy.

filament Part of a flower that supports the anther.

food group Set of foods containing a lot of one substance that you need – carbohydrates, for example.

freezing point The temperature at which a liquid starts to freeze.

fruit Part of a plant formed from a flower that contains seeds.

gas State of matter in which the matter flows easily, can change shape easily, and can change volume easily (can be squashed into a smaller space).

germinate When a shoot and root start to grow out of a seed.

gram (g) Unit for measuring mass.

heart Part of your body that pumps blood.

helium A gas used to make balloons float.

illegal Banned by law.

kilogram (kg) Unit for measuring mass.

life cycle Stages in an organism's life.

line graph Graph that shows how things change using a line.

liquid State of matter in which the matter flows, can change shape easily, but cannot change volume (can't be squashed into a smaller space).

lungs Parts of your body that allow you to breathe.

mass A measure of how much matter something is made of.

matter Everything is made of matter.

medicine Drug used to help people with illnesses.
melting point The temperature at which a solid starts to melt.
natural gas A gas that we use to cook with and heat our homes.
nicotine Addictive drug found in tobacco.
nitrogen A gas in the air, used to fill crisp packets.
observations What you see happening in an investigation.
orbit The path that an object takes as it circles around another.
ovary Part of a flower that contains the ovum.
ovum Part of a flower that joins with part of the pollen grain to start forming a seed.
oxygen A gas in the air needed by our bodies.
pitch How high or low a sound is.
pollen Grains produced by anthers in flowers and needed for reproduction in plants.
pollen grain Part of a flower that joins with the ovum to start forming a seed.
pollen tube Tube that grows from a pollen grain to the ovum in plant reproduction.
pollination When pollen is carried from the anther of a flower to the stigma of another flower.
property What a material is like. Properties include hardness, stretchiness, squashiness and permeability.
protein Substance in some foods that you need in order to grow.
pulse A pumping feeling that can be felt on your wrist or neck, caused by your heart beating.
pulse rate (beats per minute) The number of times you can feel your pulse in one minute.
reproduce When an organism makes new organisms similar to itself.
reversible change A change that can be undone, so you end up with what you started with. Melting, freezing, evaporation and condensation are all reversible changes.
seed Part of a plant that can grow into a new plant.
sepal Thick petals that protect a flower when it is a bud.
solid State of matter in which the matter cannot flow, or change shape or volume easily (can't be squashed into a smaller space).
soundproofing Using materials to stop sound travelling from one place to another.
stamen Male parts of a flower – anther and filament.
states of matter The three different forms that matter can take – solid, liquid, gas.
steam Another word for water vapour.
stigma Part of a flower that receives pollen.
style Part of a flower that supports the stigma.
theory Scientific idea.
vibrating Moving quickly backwards and forwards.
vitamin Substance in some foods that you need a small amount of to stay healthy.
volume The amount of space that something takes up.
water cycle Water moving from seas to clouds and back to seas again by evaporation, condensation and raining.
water vapour Water as a gas.